JIMMY CARTER
Beyond the Presidency

By Mellonee Carrigan

CHILDRENS PRESS ®
CHICAGO

PHOTO CREDITS

Cover, 1, 3, 5 (both photos), 7, 9, 11, 13, 14, AP/Wide World; 17, UPI/Bettmann; 18, 19, AP/Wide World; 20, 22, UPI/Bettmann; 23, AP/Wide World; 24, Ray Sciascia/© Habitat for Humanity International; 25 (top), Reuters/Bettmann; 25 (bottom left), UPI/Bettmann; 25 (bottom right), 26, AP/Wide World; 27, UPI/Bettmann; 29, AP/Wide World; 31, Julie Lopez/© Habitat for Humanity International; 32, Charles Plant/© Habitat for Humanity International

EDITORIAL STAFF

Project Editor: Mark Friedman
Design and Electronic Composition: Biner Design
Photo Editor: Jan Izzo

Library of Congress Cataloging-in-Publication Data
Carrigan, Mellonee.
    Jimmy Carter : beyond the presidency / by Mellonee Carrigan.
        p. cm. — (Picture-story biographies)
    ISBN 0-516-04193-2
    1. Carter, Jimmy, 1924–   —Juvenile literature.
2. Presidents—United States—Biography—Juvenile literature. [1. Carter, Jimmy, 1924– . 2. Presidents.]
I. Title.   II. Series: Picture-story biographies.

E872.C365 1995
973.926′092—dc20
[B]   94-41103
                                                                CIP
                                                                 AC

JANUARY 2, 1977, was a bitterly cold day in Washington, D.C. Yet tens of thousands of Americans came out to cheer as Jimmy Carter became president of the United States. It was his inauguration day.

President Carter told Americans that he wanted to be "president of the people." He soon showed that he meant what he said. As crowds lined the streets to watch the inaugural parade, Carter told his Secret Service driver to stop the presidential limousine. With a broad smile, he grabbed his wife's hand and said, "Let's go!"

People in the crowd were astonished. They shouted, "They're walking! They're walking!"

Jimmy Carter (left) and his family walk down Washington's Pennsylvania Avenue during Carter's inaugural parade.

Americans were shocked to see the president and his wife leave their limousine and walk, just like normal people. The Carters' three sons and their wives joined them. Soon, Jimmy Carter was surrounded by his family and many friendly faces. They strolled hand in hand down the center of Pennsylvania Avenue. Jimmy Carter, once a Georgia peanut farmer, proved he would not put himself above the people.

Jimmy Carter was born on October 1, 1924, in Plains, Georgia. Plains was a farming community of less than 700 people. Jimmy's parents were James Earl and Lillian Carter. Jimmy was named after his father—his full name is James Earl Carter, Jr. He was the oldest of four children. He had two sisters, Gloria and Ruth, and one brother, William Alton Carter, known as Billy.

Jimmy's father was a farmer and businessman. His mother was a

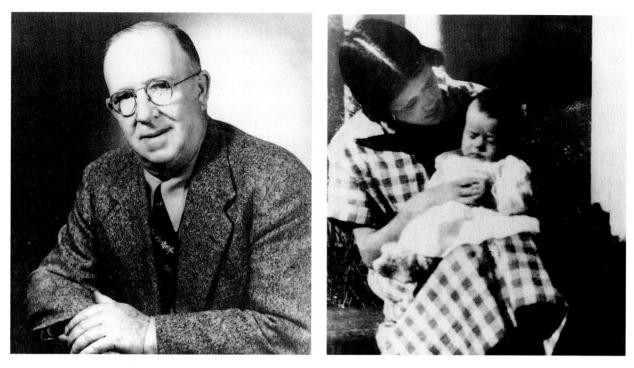

Jimmy's parents, James (left) and Lillian (right, with Jimmy as a baby)

registered nurse. He grew up in a six-room, clapboard farmhouse. The house had no electricity or indoor plumbing. Jimmy's mother cooked on a wood-burning stove. The family often read at the dinner table by kerosene light.

One of Jimmy's earliest memories is of a day when he was about four years old. He and his father were walking through the woods. They came upon a small pond about four feet deep. His father picked him up, threw him into the water, and said, "Swim, son, swim!" And that was how Jimmy learned to swim.

Jimmy was no stranger to hard work. His father worked hard and expected the same from the rest of his family. The Carters awoke before 4:00 A.M. every day for a hearty breakfast. Jimmy and his father would gather the mules by lantern light to plow the cotton, peanut, and corn fields. Farming methods on the Carter farm were quite primitive in the 1930s. The planting and plowing were done by hand.

Jimmy's father was his best friend. He taught Jimmy how to fish and hunt. They rode to and from the fields together in a wagon and talked like pals as they rode.

Jimmy was a young boy during the years of the Great Depression, which began in 1929. When the American economy collapsed, many people lost

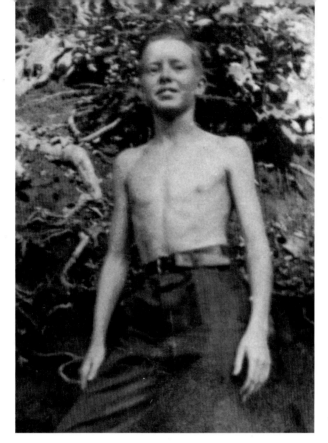

*Jimmy at age
thirteen in 1938*

their jobs. Businesses and banks failed.
People stood in long lines for food. The
Depression hit farmers hard, but the
Carter family managed to make ends
meet. The Carters had 4,000 acres of land.
They weren't rich by the world's
standards, but they weren't poor by
Sumter County, Georgia, standards.

Jimmy's father taught him to respect
money. When Jimmy was six years old,
he had his own business—selling

peanuts. He would go into the fields and pull up the peanuts, take them home, shake them out, and wash them. The next day, he and his mother would boil the peanuts and put them in small, paper bags. Jimmy would take his little wagon full of peanuts into town and sell them on the street. He made about a dollar a day, which was pretty good money during the Depression.

By the time Jimmy was ten, he wanted to expand his business. He and his older cousin, Hugh, became partners. They sold old newspapers and scrap iron, and helped his father at his store. The boys also sold hot dogs and hamburgers for a nickel apiece.

Sometimes for fun, Jimmy and his cousin would hitchhike to a nearby town and catch a double feature movie. But Jimmy's studies always came first. Reading was his favorite recreation. The family would bring books to the dinner table and read and eat in silence.

Jimmy was educated in the Plains public schools. When he grew up, he attended Georgia Southwestern College and the Georgia Institute of Technology. In 1943, his childhood dream came true. He entered the United States Naval Academy in Annapolis, Maryland. His classmates saw him as the ever-smiling "nice guy." He did especially well in electronics, gunnery, and naval tactics. He became an expert at identifying enemy ships and aircraft. He also took flying lessons.

Jimmy (kneeling at right) and friends from the Naval Academy in 1945

When Jimmy was home on leave in 1944, his sister, Ruth, brought home her best friend, Rosalynn Smith. Jimmy asked Rosalynn to go out with him. After just one date, Jimmy told his mother that Rosalynn was the girl he wanted to marry.

Jimmy received a Bachelor of Science degree from the Naval Academy in June 1946. A month later, on July 7, Jimmy and Rosalynn were married. She was almost nineteen, and he was almost twenty-two.

Jimmy spent the next eight years in the United States Navy. He served with both the Atlantic and Pacific fleets and rose to the rank of lieutenant. Jimmy and Rosalynn often were apart because Jimmy spent weeks at sea. In 1947, their first child, John William, was born. They nicknamed him Jack. They had two more sons, James Earl III (later nicknamed Chip) and Donnel Jeffrey (or Jeff).

Rosalynn (left) pins Jimmy's bars to his navy uniform as his mother, Lillian (right), watches.

In 1952, Jimmy's father became ill with cancer. He died the next year at age fifty-nine. When his father died, Jimmy felt responsible for his family. Now there was nobody to run the family farm. He resigned from the Navy and moved back to Plains, Georgia. It had been eleven years since Jimmy had worked on the farm. He decided to grow peanuts and took charge of his father's peanut warehouse. Rosalynn also worked in the family business. She kept track of the money. Sometimes Jimmy and Rosalynn worked eighteen hours a day.

Jimmy was so busy with his new responsibilities that he had little time to think of political ambitions. But he had become involved in the affairs of the community. He was so well respected by the people of Plains that friends asked him to run for the Georgia State Senate in 1962. He declined at first, but later changed his mind. He felt he needed a change. He campaigned hard and won the election.

In 1966, Carter decided to run for governor of Georgia. He entered the race late and did not have enough financial support to run a proper campaign. He lost the election, but vowed to run again in 1970.

On October 19, 1967, Jimmy and Rosalynn's only daughter, Amy Lynn, was born. Her birth was followed by

Jimmy hurries to write a speech during the 1966 governor's race.

three busy years as Jimmy planned his
next campaign for governor. Carter
made about 1,800 speeches. He wrote all
of them himself, which is unusual,
because most politicians hire people to
write their speeches.

Despite his hard work, Carter was having trouble making himself known to most voters. He decided that he must convince average working people that he was their friend and understood their problems.

He decided to make the peanut his identifying symbol. Carter's supporters wore gold peanut pins. He told voters that the peanut represented what he stood for — simple, solid values, such as hard work.

Jimmy stands in a mountain of peanuts at his family's peanut farm in Plains, Georgia.

In the November election, Carter won with sixty percent of the vote. He became Georgia's seventy-sixth governor. As governor, Carter announced that "the time for racial discrimination is over...No poor, rural, weak, or black person should ever have to bear the additional burden of being deprived of the opportunity of an education, a job, or simple justice."

Governor Carter opened jobs to many blacks in the Georgia state government. He also had the portraits of civil rights leader Martin Luther King, Jr., and other important blacks from Georgia hung in the Georgia state capitol. It was the first time a picture of a black person was allowed to appear in the capitol.

Jimmy Carter became known for his ability to get things done in government. He believed that he could accomplish great things in an even higher office. On December 12, 1974, he formally announced he would run for president of the United States. When Jimmy told his mother he was going to run for president, she said, "President of what?"

Although his mother was soon on his side, few other people took Jimmy Carter seriously. He traveled across the country making campaign speeches, but few people came to listen. Jimmy just worked harder.

Gradually, people began listening to Jimmy Carter. In 1974, the U.S. government had been rocked by scandal when President Richard Nixon resigned from office. Americans had become distrustful of government officials, and they wanted a change. Jimmy Carter's down-home, straightforward approach appealed to the voters.

In July 1976, Jimmy Carter won the Democratic Party's nomination for president. Carter stood before the convention with a wide, proud grin. He said, "Hello, my name is Jimmy Carter,

The Carter clan celebrates after Jimmy's nomination as the Democratic Party's candidate for president.

and I'm running for president of the United States." He told the cheering Democrats it was a time for healing the nation. He promised to be responsive to the people.

Jimmy Carter's message was heard. On November 2, 1976, he was elected president of the United States with 51 percent of the vote. He defeated Gerald Ford, the Republican president who was running for re-election.

During the 1978 Camp David summit, Carter meets with Menachem Begin (left) and Anwar Sadat (right).

As president, Jimmy Carter's crowning achievement was the peace treaty he negotiated between Egypt and Israel. For years, Israel had been at war with several Arab countries in the Middle East. President Carter brought Egyptian president Anwar Sadat and Israeli prime minister Menachem Begin to the United States. Carter met with them for thirteen days at the Camp David presidential retreat in the Maryland mountains. Finally, a treaty called the Camp David Accord was signed. It guaranteed peace between Israel and Egypt — a peace that lasts to this day.

President Carter also helped negotiate treaties to give back ownership of the Panama Canal to Panama. He made progress in convincing the Soviet Union to limit production of nuclear weapons. He established U.S. diplomatic relations with the communist People's Republic of China. And he supported many human rights causes throughout the world.

Carter's administration established a new program to conserve energy. He urged Americans to lower their thermostats and drive more fuel-efficient cars. Carter also created a new

President Carter and Soviet president Leonid Brezhnev exchange documents after signing an important arms-reduction treaty.

A grim President Carter meets with Secretary of State Cyrus Vance (left) during the Iran hostage crisis of 1979-80.

Department of Education. He presided over major educational and environmental protection legislation.

Near the end of his term as president, an international crisis erupted that overshadowed all of Jimmy Carter's achievements. For years, the United States had supported the government of the Shah of Iran. In 1979, the Iranian people overthrew the Shah. Anger at the Shah and the United States was running high in Iran. On November 4, 1979, armed Iranian students stormed the U.S. embassy in Tehran and took ninety people hostage, including sixty-three Americans.

President Carter demanded that the hostages be released, but the Iranian captors refused. The hostage crisis dragged on for more than a year. During this time, Jimmy Carter never left the White House. He wanted to devote his full attention to the situation in Iran. Carter then lost the 1980 presidential election to Ronald Reagan. Some political experts believe that if not for the hostage crisis, Carter might have been reelected.

On January 20, 1981, Iran released the American hostages. It was the same day Ronald Reagan was inaugurated as president. Jimmy Carter was not in Washington for the inauguration — he flew to a U.S. military hospital in West Germany to greet the freed hostages. It was a bittersweet day for Carter, now the ex-president. Carter said, "I've not achieved all I set out to do. Perhaps no one ever does."

Jimmy Carter's achievements in public service did not end when he left the White House. He published several books on politics that earned him respect as a political analyst. In 1982, he became University Distinguished Professor at Emory University in Atlanta. Together with the university, he founded the Carter Center. The Center tries to improve the quality of people's lives. It conducts programs to fight hunger in the United States, Africa, the Middle East, and Russia. It promotes health issues and fights disease. It helps revitalize urban

Jimmy Carter is joined by former president Gerald Ford (right) at a 1983 Carter Center conference.

On the blackboard and poster:

PRESIDENT JIMMY CARTER
President Carter was born and
raised in the state of Georgia.
When he grew up, the people
of Georgia elected him as their
governor.
In 1976, Jimmy Carter ran for
President of the United States.
He won!
President Carter has helped
many people throughout the
world.
He is a man of peace.
President Jimmy Carter is a
great man.

Jimmy Carter often visits schoolchildren. Much of his work involves improving education in the United States.

neighborhoods that are struggling with poverty and crime. And the Center helps promote democracy in countries where individual freedom is in peril. Through its Global 2000 program, Carter advances health and agriculture in the developing world.

In 1991, Carter launched The Atlanta Project. This program attacks social problems associated with poverty in inner cities. The program helps prevent teenage pregnancy, kids dropping out of school, juvenile delinquency, crime and violence, homelessness, drug abuse, and unemployment.

23

Jimmy Carter also became a volunteer for Habitat of Humanity. The nonprofit organization helps build homes for the needy in the United States and in other countries. Volunteers do the construction work and supply many of the building materials. This keeps the cost of the housing down. Habitat for Humanity then makes interest-free loans to families so they can buy the homes.

Jimmy and Rosalynn Carter have devoted many hours to building houses for the needy. They work with the nonprofit organization Habitat for Humanity.

Jimmy Carter regularly meets with the world's most important leaders; here, he greets Chinese premier Deng Xiaoping in 1987.

Jimmy Carter has become a trusted negotiator in troubled areas of the world. In 1989, Carter went to Panama as an official observer of that country's elections. He denounced the elections as fraudulent.

In June 1994, the former president was called upon to help settle an international crisis with North Korea. Tensions were growing between the United States and North Korea over

North Korea's nuclear program. The United States believed that North Korea was trying to build nuclear weapons. The North Koreans had removed 8,000 fuel rods from a nuclear reactor. The United States and other nations were concerned that they would use the rods to produce plutonium, a substance that can be used to make atomic bombs.

Jimmy Carter appears with four other U.S. presidents in 1991. From left to right are: George Bush, Ronald Reagan, Carter, Gerald Ford, and Richard Nixon.

When North Korea refused to allow international inspectors to see their nuclear plants, the conflict deepened. It was possible that the United States might go to war with North Korea.

The crisis was defused, however, when President Bill Clinton sent Jimmy Carter to North Korea. Carter negotiated for several days with the North Korean government. Finally, he convinced them to halt their nuclear program. Carter's negotiations paved the way to an historic treaty between the United States and North Korea that ended forty years of hostility.

Three months later, in September 1994, Carter played a key role in the clash between the United States and Haiti, a small island nation in the Caribbean.

President Clinton was about to invade Haiti in an attempt to bring down the brutal military rulers of the country. Jimmy Carter urged the president to let

Carter arrives on his emergency mission to Haiti in September 1994.

him try to end the standoff peacefully. Although previous negotiations had failed, Clinton accepted Carter's offer.

Jimmy Carter and a team of negotiators flew to Haiti, where they met with the Haitian leaders. As they negotiated, U.S. warships sat in the waters off Port-au-Prince, Haiti's capital. Carter hoped to convince the Haitian leaders that there were better options than suffering a U.S. invasion.

The negotiations were going nowhere. Carter feared an American invasion would occur within hours. With U.S. warplanes in the air and seventy-three minutes into their mission, there was a breakthrough. At the last possible moment, Carter persuaded the dictators to give up power within a month and to restore the democratic government of Haitian President Jean-Bertrand Aristide. With barely four hours to spare, the U.S. invasion was called off as Jimmy Carter struck a deal for peace in Haiti.

Carter's successful missions in North Korea and Haiti were important chapters in a long string of remarkable achievements for the ex-president. Although he was voted out of office after only one term as president, Jimmy Carter proved that there is life after the presidency. Whether wielding a

hammer and nails or negotiating in
world affairs, the "president of the
people" has continued to help all
people. Jimmy Carter has become
perhaps the most respected and
successful ex-president in the nation's
history.

JIMMY CARTER

1924   October 1 — James Earl Carter, Jr., is born in Plains, GA

1941–42   Attended Georgia Southwestern College

1942–43   Attended Georgia Institute of Technology

1943–46   Attended the United States Naval Academy and
            graduated 59th in class of 820

1946   July 7 — married Rosalynn Smith

1946–53   Served in the United States Navy

1947   Son John William (Jack) born

1950   Son James Earl III (Chip) born

1952   Son Donnel Jeffrey (Jeff) born

1953–77   Worked as farmer and warehouseman in Plains, GA

1962   Elected Georgia state senator

1966   Ran for governor of Georgia (finished third)

1967   Daughter Amy Lynn born

1970   Elected governor of Georgia

1976   Elected president of the United States

1982   Founded the Carter Center of Emory University

1991   Launched The Atlanta Project

1994   Diplomatic missions to North Korea and Haiti

INDEX

ABOUT THE AUTHOR

Mellonee Carrigan grew up in Star City, Arkansas. She attended the University of
Arkansas at Fayetteville. She received a bachelor of arts degree in journalism. Ms.
Carrigan's professional background includes work as a copy editor for *Electronic Media*
newspaper in Chicago. She was a news reporter and national broadcast news
writer/editor for United Press International in Chicago. She also was a reporter for the
City News Bureau of Chicago.

   In addition, Ms. Carrigan has written free-lance articles for the *Chicago Tribune*
newspaper and *Metro New York* magazine. She also received a certificate in television
studio production and was a 1994 graduate of the Maynard Institute for Journalism
Education's Editing Program for Minority Journalists. Ms. Carrigan's hobbies include
reading, biking and competitive running. She has completed two Chicago Marathons and numerous other
races. She presently resides in Chicago.